The Formula for Success

The Formula for Success

Bill Morris

ISBN-13: 9781546974017
ISBN-10: 1546974016
Library of Congress Control Number: 2017909029
CreateSpace Independent Publishing Platform
North Charleston, South Carolina

Dedication

I want to dedicate this book to my two sons, Christopher and Jason, who have provided me enormous happiness and couldn't be happier with their success as entrepreneurs.

I also want to dedicate this to my former wife, Cynthia, mother of my sons, and her husband Eddie. Although we have been divorced for many years, she and Eddie did a fabulous job as loving, caring and giving parents to my fabulous sons. Yes, it takes a Village.

Finally, I want to acknowledge my thousands of "adopted" kids—my students over the years at the Paul Merage School of Business at the University of California, Irvine.

Preface

There are three types of people in this world: those who make it happen, those who watch it happen, and those who say, "What happened?"

Likewise, there are different attitudes toward success. Some people think the formula for success is knowing how to make money. Such people should not buy this book. Others think the formula for success might be about investments. These people also should not buy this book (unless they view it as an investment in themselves).

But if you hope to improve yourself, increase your happiness quotient, feel better about yourself, or feel better physically, or you simply want to reaffirm that people who help the less fortunate are on the right path for success, then this book is for you.

Contents

Introduction

The two most important days
in your life are
the day you are born
and the day you find out why.

-- Mark Twain

Welcome to *The Formula for Success*. This book was created to discuss the principles, concepts, and even the game plan for how to be successful. I believe that what you are about to read will change your life for the better; it's what I call finding your "road to happy."

Over the past twenty-five years, I have assembled, structured, and produced what I believe is a winning formula that can be implemented and executed by anyone who wants success.

I have taken the things I have learned over the years in business, athletics, and parenting and put them into a formula: "The Formula for Success." This formula is grounded in the belief that we need to balance three primary disciplines: the mental, the physical, and the spiritual. If we think of life as a three-legged stool, we can see that all three legs have to be there and be in balance. Success starts with getting the mental part ignited. Once we have our heads on straight, our bodies can follow, and once we have *that* together, we can go to the advanced part—the spiritual. Keep in mind that the spiritual part uses the concepts of personal leadership and "paying it forward." Once you own this formula, the only thing I ask of you is that you help another achieve success and find happiness in this world.

The Mental

This book will show you how to build your self-esteem and self-confidence by achieving your goals and believing in yourself.

We will start with a section called "Pathways," which explains some fundamental concepts. Then we will cover time management, goal setting, PMA (positive mental attitude), and dealing with setbacks.

If you are in business, you know you can't make something happen without a strategy or marketing plan. The same applies here. You are actually going to design your own strategy, one based on your heart's desires and your plans. So, as I said, think of yourself as a business and consider what you need to be profitable.

The Physical

In order to be successful, you have to feel good both internally and externally. You also have to have the proper nutrition and the strength to compete. If you are eating the wrong things, you simply will not have the energy or desire to compete.

Nutrition is a huge part of success. As I always say, "You can't run a Ferrari on regular." You have to have the right fuel in your system to compete, and that means you have to know what the right kind of fuel is.

I am constantly approached about fitness tips and techniques in the gym. The truth is that 80 percent of success in fitness is nutrition and 20 percent is the gym.

The Spiritual

The third leg of the stool is spirituality. Somebody once asked me if my formula is faith based. It is not! It's all about leadership and helping others.

I talk to all sorts of audiences. They can be a Christian or Jew or Buddhist or Hindu—it doesn't make any difference to me how you were raised. What does make a difference is what you do for others—how you pay it forward and how you give back. Do you volunteer? How do you make other people's lives a little bit easier? Of course, to pay it forward, you need something in the bank. That's why we have to work on ourselves first. We need to make an investment in ourselves that will yield a return, and this return can then be shared with others.

Hopefully, you are excited about starting this new and improved chapter of your life. Your first question probably is, "Where do I start?"

My way of achieving success is to start with what I call the low-hanging fruit—the parts that are easier to achieve. Thus, we will cover the mental and physical sections first. The spiritual part we will cover last because this is something we give when we have something to give away.

You see, the spiritual part is about empathy, understanding, compassion, and leadership. It is your way of paying it forward, the ability to help others. This, I believe, is the true essence of life. But certain characteristics need to be created, nurtured, cultivated, grown, and developed for our own use first, before we can give to others. In other words, we have to have these things in our bag before we put our hands in and give to others.

We will start with the mind and body and can work on those sections simultaneously. In the section on the mind, we will cover pathways, time management, goal setting, dealing with setbacks, and creating a PMA, or positive mental attitude.

In the section on the body, I will show you fitness techniques you can use with or without weights, proper methods of training, ways to gain or lose weight, proper nutrition (including vitamins), and even the way to read food labels for accurate calorie content.

Foods to eat and foods to avoid will also be covered, as well as my tips and secrets for proper meal preparation.

The Road to Happy

Laughter is an instant vacation.
—JOHN MILTON

Do you ever feel that you are going through life in such a specific routine that you just are not happy? Do you feel like you are just going through the motions? Or are you totally unclear as to what the future will bring? Well, below are some things that might be in your way and some fabulous quotes and thoughts that just might inspire you to find *your* road to happy.

Eleanor Roosevelt said, "Happiness isn't a goal, it's a by-product." She also said, "No one can make you feel inferior without your consent." Often in our lives, we do not have a great support system. We may have people telling us what we can't achieve or people putting doubt into our thought processes. I consider them as individuals who want to rent negative space in your brain.

Ralph Waldo Emerson said, "For every sixty seconds you are angry, you lose a minute of happiness." Letting go of anger and negative thoughts is truly a gift to you, and it requires practice. If you decide to "rent space" in your head, make it positive. It's been said that if happy thoughts run through your mind, they will show on your face. This is why I tell my students when they enter my classroom that they have two choices: they can look like they are going to a wedding, or they can look like they are going to a funeral. My students are gifted with aptitude, but I impress upon them that it's their attitude that will be the foundation of their success and that a smile is their greatest asset. Last semester I had over eighty students from twenty-four different countries, and although there are hundreds of languages in this world, a smile speaks all of them.

I also offer you two proverbs. The first is Chinese: "Make happy those who are near and those who are far will come." The second is Turkish: "A fool dreams of wealth, but a wise man dreams of happiness." These quotes remind us that a happy person draws others together and that happiness is the essence of true wealth.

The great Dalai Lama said, "Happiness is not ready made it comes from your own actions." This is why the chapter on goal setting is so important. We need to take action to make things happen; we cannot just dream about them. Dreaming is nothing more than organizing ideas for tomorrow's actions.

Finding your passion starts the process, and taking action starts the journey. My motto in life is "Learn, earn, and return." At this point in my life, success is about giving back. Success is about your integrity—your character and your soul coming together to make this world of ours a better place.

Three great quotes I think say it all when it comes to the soul and character. The first is from Marwa Collins: "Character is what you know you are—not what others think you have." The second is from Wayne Dryer, who said, "The measure in your life will not be judged by what you accumulate but rather by what you give away." And the third is from B. D. Schiers: "If you want to change the world, start with the next person who comes to you in need."

What's Your Vision?

I saw the angel in the marble and carved until I set him free.
—MICHELANGELO

You cannot go back in time and make a brand-new start, but you can make a new start to make a brand-new ending. I sincerely believe that if you can identify your passion, you can create your vision. If you were to build a home, you would start with a great foundation. Your goals will be defined by how you structure your vision. Success starts with the thirty-five-thousand-foot view. On the heels of the creation of your vision comes your drive. Ayn Rand, author of *Atlas Shrugged* and *The Fountainhead*, said, "The question isn't who is going to let me; it's who is going to stop me."

Who Are Your Friends, and What Are Their Souls Like?

> I destroy my enemies when I make them my friends.
> —ABRAHAM LINCOLN

We know that "no man is an island." In this world we need to know how to get along with one another even if we don't see eye to eye. Bryon Katie said, "It's not your job in this world to like me, it's mine." It's said that we are judged by the company we keep, and I have often said that if two people bring the same thing to a party, one is not needed. What I mean by this is that we can be in the same church—just in a different pew. You need to surround yourself with those who reflect your soul; those who have compassion, passion, empathy, and understanding; and—most of all—those who help people who cannot possibly do anything for them. Booker Washington said, "If you want to lift yourself up, lift someone else up."

Forgiveness

> To understand everything is to forgive everything.
> —BUDDHA

I believe one of the fundamental elements of success is forgiveness. For sure, forgiving someone is easier said than done, but once you master it, you will be on your way to true success. Being angry, holding a grudge, or being hateful creates a type of airborne virus that not only affects everyone around you but, more importantly, also affects you. I think of negativity a disease that you inhale and absorb into your skin, your lungs, and your DNA. If you are holding someone down, by definition you have to be down there with that person, in the world of negativity. There is no way for success to happen while you are there. Mahatma Gandhi said, "The weak can never forgive. Forgiveness is an attribute of the strong."

If you want happiness for
        an hour — take a nap.

If you want happiness for
        a day — go fishing.

If you want happiness for
        a year — inherit a fortune.

If you want happiness for
        a lifetime — help someone else.

CHINESE PROVERB

My Journey

Let me begin by taking a few minutes to let you know my background and tell you how the creation of the Formula for Success came about.

I grew up just outside New York City, in New Jersey, but I went to high school in the Bronx, college in Boston, and graduate school in Manhattan. I worked for most of my career on Wall Street and lived in Manhattan, so I call New York home. Today I live in Irvine, California, and teach at the Paul Merage School of Business at UCI (University of California, Irvine).

My life has been very interesting. After I finished high school, I did my undergraduate work at Boston College and then my graduate work at Manhattan College in New York. My college years were tough because my mom died then. She was only in her forties, and I was the oldest of six kids, so I did the best I could to help my dad. My brothers Kenny (wife Kathy), Bobby (wife Kathy), Kevin (wife Sharon), and Mark (wife Valerie) are all beyond fabulous as is my sister Mary and her husband Bob.

After college, I was recruited to work for Exxon and had several promotions in the few years I was there. Then I was recruited to go to Wall Street and had the opportunity to work for one of the best investment banks on Wall Street, Kidder Peabody. (It no longer exists because of mergers and acquisitions.) As the international controller, I was responsible for everything internationally, in London, Paris, Geneva, Zurich, Hong Kong, and Tokyo. I also did quite a bit of traveling and got heavily involved with international issues in Tokyo and London while I was with Shearson Lehman Brothers. After that I got involved with mergers and acquisitions, which is investment banking for privately held businesses.

While I was working on Wall Street, I was married, and my two sons, Christopher and Jason, were born. I decided to help the Make-A-Wish Foundation, which at that time (the early eighties) was newly created. Not knowing if it was a legitimate business, I called the foundation and said I would like to raise money for them...but first I wanted to audit their books. When I discovered that ninety-two cents on each dollar raised reached the children, I was in.

I decided a great fund-raiser would be a push-up and sit-up contest with all the professional New York sports teams (football, baseball, hockey, and basketball). These athletes asked me what I had in mind, and when I mentioned the push-ups and sit-ups, they asked how many. When I suggested five hundred of each, they all said no. "It's not a contest," I said, "just a fund-raiser," but they still said no. It was all on me, so I created a sit-up-athon, and I was the only participant.

I have been fortunate to have been the executive vice president and chief financial officer of a New York Stock Exchange company, as well as the executive vice president of mergers and acquisitions for another NYSE company.

Today, I do motivational speaking on leadership (and sometimes fitness), and I work as an adjunct professor at the Paul Merage School of Business affiliated with UCI, where I teach strategy and entrepreneurship.

Pathways

Before you start this journey, the acquisition of some core attributes is important. We will discuss what these values are and how to make sure you have them. They include, but are not limited to, character, attitude, vision, determination, endurance, trust, and the ability to give and to help others.

Money can buy a lot of things, but what it can't buy is the above. Furthermore, when you have these attributes, they can't be stolen or repossessed: you will have them forever, and no one can take them away from you.

THINGS MONEY CAN'T BUY:

1. MANNERS
2. MORALS
3. RESPECT
4. CHARACTER
5. COMMON SENSE
6. TRUST
7. PATIENCE
8. CLASS
9. INTEGRITY
10. LOVE

Motivational Speaking

I have had the privilege of speaking to audiences across the United States. I have spoken to kids in high schools, colleges, halfway homes, drug rehab centers, continuation schools, foster homes, obesity camps, and even detention centers. I have also had the privilege to speak at West Point, Stanford University and the World Drug Conference, and I do leadership seminars for corporations.

Regardless of where I am, audiences have the same question: What does it take to be successful?

It's interesting to see that most kids have the same types of issues. They worry about having friends and being popular and are concerned about body image, grades, parents, and siblings—that kind of stuff. The last thing they think about (and the last thing I thought about at their age) is what they will be and whether they will be successful.

There are three elements that you need to get in sync to make success happen: the mental, the physical, and the spiritual. I call these the three-legged stool because if one of them is missing, the stool can't stand. This book is going to help you get these elements in sync and get your life in balance.

I always say motivational speaking is like toast—the longer it's out of the toaster, the colder it gets. So now you have a book to reference. If you are feeling down in the dumps, you can just pull this book out.

You might pull out the section on setting goals or developing a positive mental attitude, or you may reread the part about dealing with setbacks. I will be sincere, brief, and direct, which is something I learned in business. I had a boss on Wall Street who once said, "If you can't put it on the back of your business card, don't bother telling me."

Speaking at Stanford University

When I spoke at Stanford University to all the class presidents of California high schools, they said, "Bill, let's talk a little bit about peer pressure."

A young woman said, "I am class president of an all-girls school, and all the girls come into class inebriated. They come in plastered, every one of them." What do you do in that kind of situation? As a teen, you worry about having friends and being popular. You want to move with the herd because there is safety in it—you won't be singled out as a goofball. But sometimes the herd moves right into slaughter. There is no question about that.

I remember when I was a kid and my parents used to say, "If everyone was going to jump off a bridge, would you do it too?" "Yeah," I would say, "I would jump off the bridge." I knew that would get them ticked. But looking back at that exchange is interesting. As a kid, I was thinking that my parents didn't really get me. My *peers* got me, and that's why I hung out with them.

Parents chat about issues that are pure and chaste. They don't really understand what kids are going through. A kid is thinking, "I have to be popular—I have to have friends," and when that is your mind-set, you have to live and die by the herd. If the herd is doing good things, that is one thing, but if the herd is doing bad things, you have to sign up for that as well.

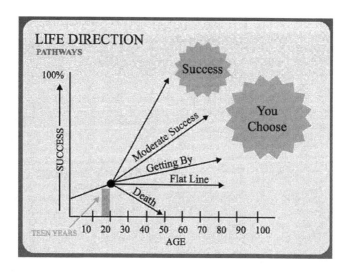

My advice to that young woman was that she needed to stand alone.

Negative Life Experiences

Life-changing events will always come into our lives, events that alter what we thought we knew. As a result, we may lose some compassion, some empathy, and some kindness, and we will certainly lose some of our innocence.

The September 11th, 2001 terrorist attacks in New York City were debilitating to me in many ways because I had worked on Wall Street. I worked on Broad Street, I worked on Broadway right by the New York Stock Exchange, and I worked in the World Trade Center. I had an office on the 102nd floor and had to take three elevators to get to my office. For many years, that was my home, and so the attack hit very, very close.

The son of a dear friend of mine was right there when the plane entered the building. He was the same age as my boys, and his death was devastating—and still is to this day.

Life, like a roller coaster, has ups and downs. Although that fateful day was for sure a negative life-altering event, I want to give you the gift of a positive life-altering event—the Formula for Success.

Positive Life Experiences

My hope for you today is that as you read this book, you will have a positive life experience. Even if it is something small, I am confident that it will provide you with the opportunity to move in a positive direction.

Faucets

If you are standing in front of a sink and you extend both arms toward the faucet, you can reach the hot just as easily as you can reach the cold.

Now think of one of those faucets as a PMA, or positive mental attitude, and the other as an NMA, or negative mental attitude. Just like with the faucets, it is as easy to reach one as it is to reach the other.

Every day we have a choice. Choose the positive.

Money Is Good

We are going to cover the concepts of success and how to be successful. One thing I want you to understand is that success is really not about money. Now, money is good; I like money. In fact, the more I have, the more I can give away.

I am from Wall Street, where we always think that money is a good thing, but money doesn't bring happiness.

The definition of success for me personally is being able to set moral and ethical goals and being able to achieve them.

The Key to Success

What is the cornerstone of success? If I have to use one noun, its *attitude*, and if I have to use one adjective, it's *nonjudgmental*. To me, the latter is probably one of the most important words in the whole world.

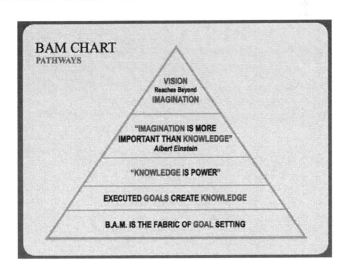

Hotel California

We all know people involved with drugs, alcohol, and the like. In such cases, it is important to be nonjudgmental and take a step back. That's their inventory, but that doesn't mean it is your inventory. You don't always know the journey someone has been on, so don't judge.

Why do people turn to drugs and alcohol? I've been speaking to all types of groups, from high-school kids to corporate executives, for about twenty-five years, and I think there are two primary reasons.

1. They don't lead—they follow. This is the herd mentality: they want to be with the herd because they want to be accepted by their peers. Somebody probably said, "Let's go smoke" or "Let's go drink." Someone—I wouldn't consider such people friends—brought them in. The receiving person doesn't want to rock the boat and wants to please others.
2. They are depressed and want to check out, sometimes temporarily and sometimes permanently. Drugs and alcohol provide what I refer to as the numbing effect.

Strength is not always easy to achieve. The earlier you can learn to walk to your own beat, the better off you will be. Total success is helping others, not hurting others.

A desire for the numbing effect, as I call it, comes from a lack of goals and aspirations. For some people, no one in their lives has motivated them—no one has ever believed in them. They never knew about a formula that could help guide them.

The whole purpose of this book is to help you have an action plan in your possession that will allow you to map out a path toward success. Nobody's action plan is perfect the first time, but hopefully, your action plan will lay down some fundamentals that will propel you toward success.

My 95/5 Rule

I always say that 95 percent of people will not be successful and 5 percent will. The 95 percent have certain characteristics, and the 5 percent have other specific characteristics. These are provided in the chart above. Maybe this is why there is a "highway to hell" and only a "stairway to heaven."

Remember the faucet, and reach for the right side.

Behavior/Attitude/Mental Toughness (BAM Chart)

PATHWAYS

95%	5%
NON SUCCESSFUL ATTRIBUTES	SUCCESSFUL ATTRIBUTES
Dark	Light
Negative	Positive
Threat	Opportunity
Surviving	Living
Failure	Success
Fear	Faith/Hope
Hatred	Love
Anger	Compassion
Greed	Sympathy
Jealousy	Optimism
Lazy	Proactive
Revenge	Loyalty
Blame	Responsible
Rejection	Acceptance

Kids Have Their Own DNA

When my oldest son graduated from college, he said, "Dad, I need a job." I had a few connections, and—long story short—I helped him get a job on the floor of the New York Stock Exchange. I was so happy. He was just a runner, but it was a job!

Ninety days later, he called and said, "Dad, I have some good news and some bad news." As a parent, your heart sinks when you hear those words. I told him to give me the bad news first.

"Dad, I just quit my job at the New York Stock Exchange."

I thought we must have had a bad connection. I'm sure I had that deer-in-the-headlights look. After a period of disbelief and a ten-minute tirade about how I had pulled strings, I stopped. "Wait," I said. "You said you had some good news."

"Yes. You know how you always say I should follow my dreams and follow my goals?"

"Yes! Yes, yes," I said, excited.

"Well," my son said, "I just joined a rock-and-roll band."

After I got off the floor from my heart attack (kidding), we had a "CTJ" talk. In New York City speak, this means "Come to Jesus." I just wanted to know how he planned to eat and pay rent—two things I am very fond of. Next, we talked about setting goals: having a day job (he fixed computers and printers) and doing his music at night. And after that, success was just around the corner.

His DNA was formed even as a small child.

You know, it is funny. One day when my son and I were out for a drive, he said, "Dad, can I have that quarter on the dashboard?"

I looked over at him. "Sure," I said. I think he was about five years old. As we drove a little farther, I turned to him and said, "What do you want with the quarter?"

"I want to use it for college," he responded.

I smiled. "That's terrific," I said. "Cool." After driving a little farther, I turned to him and asked, "Where do you want to go to college?"

He turned to me and said, "I'm going to go to Clown College!" I just cracked up.

Obviously as a dad, you never forget certain things. That son is now a college graduate and a successful entrepreneur. He also is the lead singer of a great rock band that has cut an album.

My other son, who was about seven years old at the time, had a different perspective on life. One day while I was driving, I explained to him my Formula for Success and how I was going to share it with the youth of America. My son thought about that for a minute and then turned to me and said, "Dad, if you give out the Formula for Success to your audiences, will there be any room at the top for me?"

One Saturday I brought my younger son to my office on Wall Street, and, at eight years old, he insisted on bringing a briefcase. He already knew what he wanted to do in his world. Today, this son, a college graduate, is a successful real-estate developer.

Control What You Can Control, and Don't Worry about What You Can't

This book will have you focusing on what you can control. Someone asked me once if there were certain attributes one must have in order to make things happen. Yes! I call these attributes my two P's, my two D's, and my two H's.

The two P's are *persistence* and *patience*. The two D's are *desire* and *determination*. And the two H's are *habit* and *hard work*.

"Those are beautiful words," you might be thinking, "but I am not sure where to begin or how to start this thing." Don't worry. I'm going to show you how to use those words.

The Iditarod Race

The Iditarod is dogsled race that goes from Anchorage to Nome, Alaska, and it takes weeks. Close your eyes and imagine what this race is all about: there are all these dogs, and then you, in the sled.

There is an expression I use: "The view only changes for the lead dog." I think you can picture what the view is for all the other huskies.

We are here to make sure that you are the lead dog. That is where the view changes; that is where you can begin to make it toward that 5 percent. And believe me—anyone can have this. It is not brain surgery. It is a matter of understanding the formula and employing it.

Numbers Game

Let me show you another chart. In the world of business and finance, we have an expression: "It is a numbers game." For example, in sales, if you talk to one hundred people, ten will be interested, and three will buy. That is the numbers game. It is no different for you guys in the world of success: it is a numbers game. Remember the 95/5 rule.

When I speak to corporations regarding their sales efforts, stats still prevail.

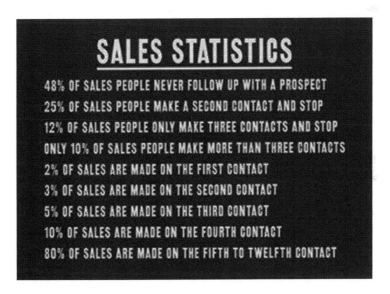

SALES STATISTICS

48% OF SALES PEOPLE NEVER FOLLOW UP WITH A PROSPECT

25% OF SALES PEOPLE MAKE A SECOND CONTACT AND STOP

12% OF SALES PEOPLE ONLY MAKE THREE CONTACTS AND STOP

ONLY 10% OF SALES PEOPLE MAKE MORE THAN THREE CONTACTS

2% OF SALES ARE MADE ON THE FIRST CONTACT

3% OF SALES ARE MADE ON THE SECOND CONTACT

5% OF SALES ARE MADE ON THE THIRD CONTACT

10% OF SALES ARE MADE ON THE FOURTH CONTACT

80% OF SALES ARE MADE ON THE FIFTH TO TWELFTH CONTACT

So Many Choices

Education is the key to success, and it doesn't matter where you get this education.

First and foremost, you have to believe in yourself. You have to believe in what you are all about. It is just that simple: you either believe or you don't; there really isn't much in between.

People often tell me that it is pretty cool that I've had a career on Wall Street and as an athlete. "What a great resume," they say.

My response is, "If you think that is impressive, you should see my list of failures. That list is much longer."

We all have setbacks. Whether or not you succeed comes down to how you react to them. Do you freak out and quit, or do you embrace them and learn from them? More on that later in the chapter on setbacks.

Education Equals Skills, and Skills Equal Paychecks

As I have said, you need a plan for success, and part of that formula is to accumulate knowledge. So that is what this section is about—accumulating knowledge. When you graduate from high school, trade school, college, or whatever you are going to do, in order to get a paycheck for goods and services, you've got to have a knowledge base. Someone's got to pay you for something you know how to do.

You can be an accountant, a lawyer, a doctor, a plumber, or a construction worker—it doesn't matter. You have to have a knowledge base to get a paycheck. Not everyone is designed for college; that's just the way it is. And not everyone is designed for trade school; it is all very specialized.

Story about Two of My Brothers

I tell this story often on stage. It is about two of my brothers. (I have four fabulous brothers and one terrific sister.)

One of my brothers went to Harvard, and another brother did not go to college. What these two have in common, however, is that both are very successful.

My brother who didn't go to college is in the construction field. He is a builder—a very successful builder. He got an education on the job. So don't think that I am pushing college—I am not. That is not what success is about. If college is for you, great. If it's not, that's great as well. But for sure you need an education to provide goods and services to get a paycheck.

Just for the record, as I mentioned previously, I was involved with middle-market M&A (mergers and acquisitions) deals.

Well, I had the good fortune to be involved in over one hundred closed M&A transactions. What this means is that we represented sellers of privately held companies. These companies ranged from $5 million to $100 million.

I have helped over one hundred clients become liquid millionaires—95 percent of them did not have college degrees. In fact, some never finished high school.

My point is that these entrepreneurs (entrepreneurship, by the way, is a subject I teach at UCI) never had a plan B. They were all driven and focused on succeeding.

View Yourself as a Corporation or a Company

The mental part of the formula is setting up the mind and the belief system. You are the one who is going to be incorporated. Think of yourself as a business. Profitability is what all businesses want. This particular plan is going to go through various phases. You Incorporated.

Speaking to Corporations

When we are managing complex change, we need all to be on the same page with our vision.

If railroad tracks that are a few degrees off from parallel: by the time you are a mile down the road, you are off several feet.

The next major "must-have" is skill. Then come incentives, and then resources, and, finally, a good action plan.

In the chart below, note that once you are blocked out (indicated by a dark box), you experience the result after the equal sign.

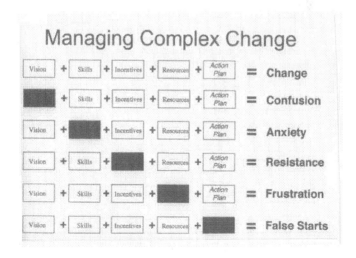

Vision
Sometimes your vision is not effectively communicated!

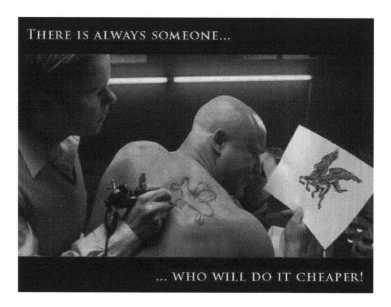

Time Management

The formula begins with the proper allocation of time, our one true asset. Regardless of your age, you need proper time allocation to achieve your goals. And this time allocation must be reserved on your time-management chart as well as in alignment with your goal chart.

In my world, you are either spending or investing your time.

Every individual will see these categories a little differently. For example, investing to me can be work time: working on a business plan, analyzing investments, developing a leadership team, going to school—anything that will increase my capital or net worth.

Spending, on the other hand, is relaxation: playing golf, reading the paper, eating, driving to work—you get the point.

Then there are the gray areas. For example, I think of talking with my students or kids as spending time; however, I also see it as an investment because it will build a better partnership and strengthen the family (which should be part of your goal chart). Keep in mind that you need both—spending *and* investing.

A time-management chart is simply the twenty-four hours of the day divided into what you spend and what you invest. For example, of the twenty-four hours, let's allocate eight for proper sleep. The remaining sixteen hours we will work with as to whether we spend or invest, and adjust accordingly. It is crucial to reallocate if your goals are not being met.

For argument's sake, let's say your division of spending and investing is even—eight and eight—but your goals are not being met. You might want to adjust or reallocate your chart so that the ratio is eleven and five. What you have done is made a commitment to increasing your investing hours to eleven (from eight) and decreasing your spending to five (from eight).

I know creating this type of chart will be new and maybe even a little strange for you, but until you take a look at yourself as a business (You Inc.), you could be out of control with your spending. I can assure you that the person you work for has a good idea of his or her spending. Why shouldn't you? Aren't you more important?

When you get time management under control, you become a better you, which in turn will make you a better worker or entrepreneur, not to mention a better spouse and parent. You also become a better friend and a more productive member of society. This is the beginning of your journey on the road to happy.

Goal Setting

My First Real Fitness Goal

When I was thirty-three years old, I set a two-year (long-term) goal for myself. This goal was to complete thirty-five hundred consecutive sit-ups on my thirty-fifth birthday.

On my thirty-fifth birthday, I went to the gym at 4:30 a.m. and began the feat. It was lonely; I was the only one there. I laid down a matchstick for every one hundred sit-ups I did until I had thirty-five matchsticks. Well, by 7:00 a.m., my goal was accomplished! I trained hard for two years, and I felt fantastic.

The Creation of the Sit-up-athon

I went to my chairman at Kidder Peabody, Al Gordon, and said, "I'm going to create a sit-up-athon, and for every sit-up I do, I would like you to donate a dollar, to the Make-A-Wish Foundation."

He said yes!

Al and I talked for about fifteen minutes, and as I was walking out of his office, I realized he hadn't asked me how many sit-ups I planned to do.

I turned to him and said, "Al, you never asked me how many I was going to attempt."

"Oh, how many," he asked.

I said, "Five thousand."

He didn't even blink. "Great! Good luck!" For Al this was coffee money.

That first year, Al was my only sponsor.

I did five of these fund-raising events over five years. In the first year, I did five thousand sit-ups, and in the second year, I did ten thousand. In years three and four,

I did fifteen thousand and then twenty thousand, and then I actually did twenty-five thousand! (I don't talk of that year much because that was the year I took a couple of "potty breaks.") But the five, ten, fifteen, and twenty thousand were all consecutive. I ended up setting a world record for consecutive sit-ups: I did twenty thousand and one hundred in eleven hours and thirty-two minutes.

Sometimes Excuses Get in the Way

Not in the Bathroom

Funny personal note here: The reason for the extra hundred sit-ups (twenty thousand and one hundred instead of twenty thousand) is that right when I completed the twenty thousand sit-ups; TV cameras from ABC, NBC, and CBS were coming in to film me and needed setup time. The extra hundred was my way to keep moving and not be interviewed in the bathroom! I had to pee so bad that I made a beeline to the potty when the interview was done. I think I spoke in short, quick sentences.

A lot of folks ask me, "How on earth did you do that?"

Of course, I responded with a joke, "Drugs and mirrors."

I sincerely believe we are capable of so much if we believe in ourselves and don't let others influence us in a negative way.

I do believe that you can do anything you set your mind to, but many elements have to come together and be in balance to make it happen.

Do You Have Dreams?

Do any of you have dreams?

This is a question I always ask my audiences. After most raise their hands, I say, "Dreams are BS!"

Once I have their attention, I explain that dreams and goals are very similar, except for one critical element: goals have target dates for completion, while dreams are just dreams.

It is my opinion that 95 percent of the people on the planet are not successful. It is also my opinion that none of these unsuccessful people have a goal-setting process.

Let's talk about the goal-setting process and my ten-step goal-setting chart.

The first step is to figure out what it is you want to achieve, why you want to achieve this objective, where and when you expect to achieve this goal (this will tie in with your time management), and how you expect to achieve it. What you need is some real alone time.

SETTING GOALS
GOAL SETTING

**DREAMS AND GOALS ARE SIMILAR, EXCEPT GOALS HAVE
TARGET DATES FOR COMPLETION**

- Successful people have them
- They are created in the NOW (present)
- They are written down and posted
- They are Long Range & Short Range
- Should not be constructed on "Fear Basis"
- Adjustments should be implemented
- Should be Realistic and Attainable

```
GOAL SETTING PROCESS
GOAL SETTING

1.  What, Why, Where, When & How
2.  Realistic & Attainable
3.  Be Decisive: In/Out
4.  Focus -- Write them down and post them
5.  Plan Properly -- Give vs. Give Up
6.  Involve Positive People
7.  Take Action: Setbacks will Happen
8.  Evaluate Progress -- shelf life not forever
9.  Reward Yourself
10. Always Maintain Integrity
```

Everything is practice, so the first time you do this, it is probably going to be horrible. The second time, it will suck, and probably by the third time, it will work. But you have to practice goal setting and time management together. Practice, practice, practice. That's what I did.

I sat and actually visualized what I really wanted out of life and what was important to me, and then I put down my goals. In my Success seminars, I always ask the audience if they have a "goal card" in their pocket. I'm not talking about American Express; I'm talking about an actual card with goals written on it.

In the twenty-one-day action plan provided in the last chapter, before the Conclusion, you will have the opportunity to practice putting your goals on paper. The goal card is part of the Formula for Success; in order to achieve your goals, you need to see in writing what you desire and what and when it will manifest. You are making a commitment by writing it down.

If you ask any young woman, "Would you rather have your boyfriend call you on the phone and tell you how much he loves you or have your boyfriend write you a beautiful poem or write a song for you to tell you how much he loves you?" she will take the second. Why? Simple: it's written down in stone, as they say, and it can be reflected upon daily. That is step four in the goal-setting process chart, and it is step number three in the setting goals chart: write them down.

Goals must be realistic and attainable. For example, if you are in your fifties, trying for a starting position in the NFL is probably not realistic or attainable. Goals also need to be broken down into short-range goals (one year or less) and long-range goals.

You have to be decisive. Do you want this to happen, or do you not want it to happen? If you are wishy-washy, it is not going to happen. You have to be committed. Not involved—committed. It's like the old joke: If you and I were at breakfast, I would say, "Look at your bacon and eggs. The chicken was involved, but the pig was committed."

You will be in the 5 percent of people on this planet who are successful if you follow these guidelines. It is a very small circle of people, and it is designed to be small. That's the way life is.

By now you know that goals have to be written down. I believe this is the most important step because it reflects commitment and acknowledgment.

There is another aspect of writing them down: you have to post them so you can see them. It may sound goofy, but I post mine on my lamp. Why do I post them there? Because it is the last thing I see before I go to bed and the first thing I see in the morning. To be in the 5 percent, you need to do this!

I can't stress enough the importance of writing down your goals and posting them where you can see them.

The next step is to determine what you are going to give and what you are going to give up. This step is huge, and it goes back to your time-management program. If you are watching three hours of TV a night and are looking to improve your financial situation, you will have to adjust your ratio of spending to investing.

I had a young man ask me if he could have the formula for how to beat my sit-up record. "Sure," I said. "I'll show you how to do it. If you can taste it, you can have it. If you can't, it is not going to happen. It's going to start with getting up at five in the morning," as I began what was required he started to "moonwalk" on me right there.

You have to plan properly because setbacks occur. For me, they happen six or seven times before I get a hit.

Involve positive people in your goal process. I don't think any success happens by itself. We need other people to make things happen, people who can bring different things to the party. Bring people who have complementary traits and are positive. Remember the 95/5 rule. That is what you always have to focus on. The 5 percent are the ones you want to seek. As for the 95 percent, you want to let them go (while being nonjudgmental). That is just the way it is.

You've got to take action and evaluate your progress; this is huge. Remember what I said earlier: Goals and dreams are similar, but goals have target dates attached to them. If you don't have a date, it is open-ended and will never have a sense of urgency to be completed. Be decisive. Know what you want and when you are going to accomplish it.

Reward yourself. When you do something good, you have to pat yourself on the back. This is very important. Say, "Hey, look—I was able to accomplish something." You may not have a good network of motivating people in your life, so you have to take care of yourself. You are incorporated for yourself. You just have to remember to think of yourself as a business. Reward yourself.

Always, always, have integrity. People love to be around positive people; it is just a natural thing. They are probably saying, "I hope some of that rubs off on me!" If you always have integrity, high morals, and ethics, you can never go wrong. Always operate from the heart—the point that is so special—to be morally and ethically right.

One of my goals, still waiting to be achieved, is to be a contestant on the television show—*The Next American Ninja Warrior*. NBC actually contacted me, and I have been in conversations with their casting crew, which suggested a "walk-on" status. So, I went up to Venice and waited on the line of one hundred, for eight hours. They never got to us. Still trying—see below.

Dealing with Setbacks

n life we all have many more setbacks than we do successes. The challenge is to know how to handle the setbacks and what to do from there.

For me, when a setback occurs, I'm expecting it, so the shock factor is nonexistent. This reduces my stress tremendously. The first thing I do is smile because, like an invited friend, I knew it was coming. Smiling also leads to less stress. Next I analyze what went wrong, learn from it, and go back and try again in a more relaxed state. As I said, this will happen several times until you get it right.

One of the biggest factors here is how we mentally prepare for setbacks. Stress makes a setback worse—much worse.

Let's go to the SARAH chart. The first three letters, which stand for *shock*, *anger*, and *rejection*, represent the dead zone. The key to success is determining how quickly you can get out of this zone.

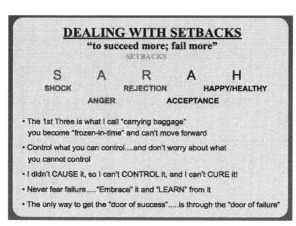

DEALING WITH SETBACKS
"to succeed more; fail more"
SETBACKS

S	A	R	A	H
SHOCK		REJECTION		HAPPY/HEALTHY
	ANGER		ACCEPTANCE	

• The 1st Three is what I call "carrying baggage"
  you become "frozen-in-time" and can't move forward

• Control what you can control....and don't worry about what
  you cannot control

• I didn't CAUSE it, so I can't CONTROL it, and I can't CURE it!

• Never fear failure....."Embrace" it and "LEARN" from it

• The only way to get the "door of success"....is through the "door of failure"

The Mind-Body Connection

Your body responds to the way you think, feel, and act. This is often called the mind-body connection. When you are stressed, anxious, or upset, your body tries to tell you that something isn't right.

For example, high blood pressure or a stomach ulcer might develop after a particularly stressful event, such as the death of a loved one. The following can be physical signs that your emotional health is out of balance:

- back pain
- change in appetite
- chest pain
- constipation or diarrhea
- dry mouth
- extreme tiredness
- general aches and pains
- headaches
- high blood pressure
- insomnia (trouble sleeping)
- light-headedness
- palpitations (the feeling that your heart is racing)
- sexual problems
- shortness of breath
- stiff neck
- sweating
- upset stomach
- weight gain or loss

Poor emotional health weakens your body's immune system, making you more likely to get colds and other infections during emotionally difficult times. I have not been sick in twenty years, and I believe that's because I don't let poor emotional health affect me.

Also, when you are feeling stressed, anxious, or upset, you may not take care of your health as well as you should. You may not feel like exercising, eating nutritious foods, or taking medicine that your doctor prescribes. Abuse of alcohol, tobacco, or other drugs may also be a sign of poor emotional health.

You may not be used to talking to your doctor about your feelings or problems in your personal life. But he or she can't always tell that you're feeling stressed, anxious, or upset just by looking at you. It's important to be honest with your doctor if you are having these feelings.

First, he or she will need to make sure that other health problems aren't causing your physical symptoms. If your symptoms aren't caused by other health problems, you and your doctor can address the emotional causes of your symptoms. Your doctor may suggest ways to treat your physical symptoms while you work together to improve your emotional health.

If your negative feelings don't go away and are so strong that they keep you from enjoying life, it's especially important for you to talk to your doctor. You may have major depression. Depression is a medical illness that can be treated with individualized counseling, medicine, or both.

Below are some ways to improve your emotional and mental health.

First, try to recognize your emotions and understand why you are having them. Sorting out the causes of sadness, stress, and anxiety in your life can help you manage your emotional health. The following are some other helpful tips.

Express your feelings in appropriate ways. If feelings of stress, sadness, or anxiety are causing physical problems, keeping these feelings inside can make you feel worse. It's OK to let your loved ones know when something is bothering you; however, keep in mind that your family and friends may not be able to help you deal with your feelings appropriately. At these times, ask someone outside the situation—such as your family doctor, a counselor, or a religious adviser—for advice and support to help you improve your emotional health.

Put your life into balance. Try not to obsess over the problems at work, school, or home that lead to negative feelings. This doesn't mean you have to pretend to be happy when you feel stressed, anxious, or upset—it's important to deal with these negative feelings—but try to focus on the positive things in your life. You may want to use a journal to keep track of things that make you feel happy or peaceful. Research has shown that having a positive outlook can improve your quality of life and give your health a boost. You may also need to let go of things in your life that make you feel stressed and overwhelmed so that you can make time for things you enjoy.

Develop resilience. If you can develop resilience, you will be able to cope with stress in a healthy way. Resilience can be learned and strengthened with different strategies. These include having social support, keeping a positive view of yourself, accepting change, and keeping things in perspective.

Practice mind and body relaxation. Relaxation methods such as meditation are useful ways to bring your emotions into balance. Meditation is a form of guided thought. It can take many forms. For example, you may do it by exercising, stretching, or breathing deeply. Ask your family doctor for advice about relaxation methods.

Consider yourself number one. This is not an ego thing. Remember, I think ego stands for "edging God out."

If your flight hits turbulence and the oxygen masks drop, what does the pilot say? "Put yours on first." The same goes for life. How can you possibly help another if you are not together?

Take care of your body. To have good emotional health, it's important to have a regular routine for eating healthy meals, getting enough sleep, and exercising to relieve pent-up tension. Avoid overeating, and don't abuse drugs or alcohol. Using drugs or alcohol just causes other problems, often with your family and your health.

Positive Mental Attitude

The mind is powerful, so guide it toward a PMA (positive mental attitude) not an NMA (negative mental attitude).

Remember my analogy about the faucets: your arms can reach both hot and cold, and each is easy to engage. It's your choice, so why not go positive?

You wanted the formula. Well, the most important muscle in the body is the brain; it starts everything. Initially, it's our attitude (light or dark) that starts this journey and, like a railroad track, takes us in a specific direction.

A positive mental attitude is the foundation of a great attitude. You might be totally suited up with a great attitude, but outside forces (like people without this shared concept) can throw you off. Like it or not, the brain is attached to the ears. We listen and are easily influenced. It's up to us to either buy in or opt out.

> In life, you will realize there is a role for everyone you meet. Some will test you, some will use you, some will love you, and some will teach you. But the ones who are truly important are the ones who bring out the best in you. They are the rare and amazing people who remind you why it's worth it. - Unknown

My Last Negative Influencer

I'll tell you a little story. As you know, for five years in a row, I created and did a sit-up-athon to raise funds for the Make-A-Wish Foundation. The first year I did five thousand sit-ups, and the second year I announced I was going to do ten thousand sit-ups.

I was training very, very hard. I used a forty-five-pound Olympic weight on my chest while doing the sit-ups, which I still work out with to this day. Well, positive mental attitude or not, a guy comes up to me and says, "You realize you are going from five thousand to ten thousand, which means you are going to double it! How is that possible? You'll never be able to do that!"

For twenty-four hours, I had doubt because I let a negative individual rent space in my head.

I had to do a little moonwalk. That was the day I first acquired my positive mental attitude. I thought, "Hey, this is only a couple thousand more—no big deal. I train a little bit harder, eat a little better, and so on. No big deal." But his comments actually affected me. When someone puts a negative thought inside your head, it's like a virus, and that's when you realize that negative people cannot rent space in your head.

What I did was to immediately say, "Thank you for your concern, but you don't know me. You don't know how driven I am, how hard I work." I employed my first rule of success: be nonjudgmental. I took his comments in, gave a little smile, and said OK. "You really don't understand me," I thought to myself. "That's not going to be a problem."

When I did the five thousand, it took me about three hours. The ten thousand took about six hours. I was right on a pace. His doubt didn't affect me whatsoever. But in order to succeed, I had to mentally drop people who had any kind of negative attitude.

In other words, if someone from the 95 percent puts a negative thought in your mind, just flush it. These people are all over the place. Don't let their viruses affect you! Remember—you are incorporated. You are a corporation. You make your decisions based on what you want. Your success is totally up to you. Remember what we said about the herd mentality and moving with the herd—you usually are heading to the slaughter. You have to ask yourself, "Is that herd really moving in the direction of my goals?"

They say the past is history, the future is a mystery, and today is a present, so you should open it like one. True mental success arrives in the present. That is where the 5 percent—the successful people—reside.

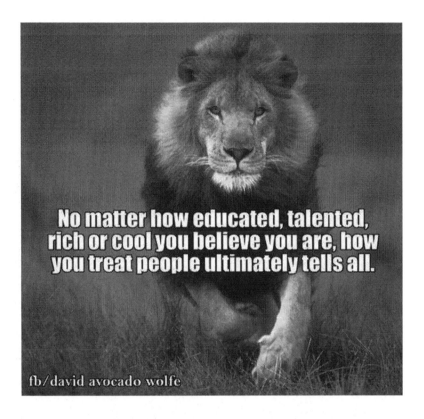

No matter how educated, talented, rich or cool you believe you are, how you treat people ultimately tells all.

fb/david avocado wolfe

For you it has arrived today—now. Most people (the other 95 percent) live in the past, in past beliefs and events. Something that happened in your past can affect your future if you don't change. If you think you can't change, you are actually programming yourself negatively, and in the future, you won't be able to adjust in a positive manner.

Henry Ford once said, "If you think you can do it you are probably right. If you think can't do it you're probably right."

For me success is about how you set the brain. There are two buttons: one says, "I can't do it," and the other says, "I *can* do it!" You have the opportunity to press either button or turn either faucet. Both are free!

Everything is practice. The best way I have found to get a PMA working in the mind is to have some small successes. In the section on goal setting, I said that your goals should be realistic and attainable. I should add that they should be small and easy to achieve.

There are "givers" and there are "receivers" in life. Maya Angelou has it right when she says, don't be a "giver" when the one you are giving to doesn't treat you in the same manner.

Take another look at my BAM chart (page 23): behavior, attitude, and mental toughness. A lot of times, we are not 100 percent sure of where we are going or what we are doing.

You have to develop that for yourself, just as an athlete develops his or her body.

BAM is the fabric of goal setting. This pyramid (page 23) is the core foundation.

It provides a vision of where you want to be, where you want to end up. You clearly define exactly what you want to achieve in your life.

Let's look at my 95/5 BAM chart (page 25). The difference between the 95 percent and the 5 percent is what I refer to as the difference between actors and reactors. Most people are reactors. They don't take action. Remember, if you really want to be successful in this world, there are three types of people: those who make it happen, those who watch it happen, and those who say, "What happened?" The people who make it happen are acting it out. They are making it happen (see these attributes under the 5 percent).

These are some of the characteristics that I run across in people I want to hang out with. These are people who come from the light not the dark. They are positive, not negative. They think of opportunities rather than looking at the threats.

A great question I ask is, "Are you living or are you surviving?"

Friend selection is of utmost importance. You don't want enablers; you want those who believe in you and can encourage you toward success.

Spiritual Leadership

N ow let's talk about the third leg of the stool: spirituality.
I was asked in one of my seminars if this leg was faith based—it's not. It's about leadership and helping others, so it is spiritual. My audiences are people who are Jewish, Christian, Muslim, Buddhist, and so on. There are so many faiths, cultures, and religions in this world. In fact, I recently looked up how many organized religions there are and was surprised to find out that there are over forty-four hundred.

The Leadership Principles

The leadership qualities you want to develop are on the BAM chart (page 25), which starts with coming from the light or being nonjudgmental.

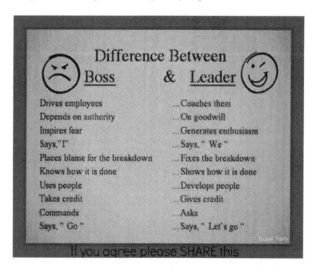

Difference Between Boss	& Leader
Drives employees	...Coaches them
Depends on authority	...On goodwill
Inspires fear	...Generates enthusiasm
Says,"I"	...Says, " We "
Places blame for the breakdown	...Fixes the breakdown
Knows how it is done	...Shows how it is done
Uses people	...Develops people
Takes credit	...Gives credit
Commands	...Asks
Says, " Go "	...Says, " Let's go "

If you agree please SHARE this

Quite simply, the spiritual part of success is about giving back to others. I don't believe you can actually give back to others until you are complete and whole yourself. This is why we save this for last. Once you become complete and are happy with you, then you are prepared to give to others. I always say that you cannot really love another person until you really love yourself. What would you have to give? You've got to be happy with who you are as an individual.

The Soup Kitchen

I found the best way to discover how to give back is through understanding, empathy, and compassion, and for me, volunteer work at the aforementioned soup kitchen is my Formula for Success.

Lao Tse was a sixth-century philosopher, and he said a leader is one who serves. When I was in New York City, I spent a lot of time—my Sunday mornings, actually—at Saint Francis Xavier Soup Kitchen, which is down on Fifteenth Street in Lower Manhattan. I would take my boys with me as well.

Honestly, I never feel as complete as I do when I am helping other people. The people who come in for a meal are stripped of self-esteem; they are stripped of self-confidence. They have tremendous difficulty making eye contact. They are down and out and down on their luck. There is no question about it. As I stated before, what you want to do is be in that kind of environment, helping people who are not as fortunate as you. As we would serve meals to these individuals, they would look up meekly and thank us with their eyes. For me as an individual, this completes who I am. As I said earlier, my motto in life is "Learn, earn, and return." The art of "paying it forward is to give to those less fortunate."

The concepts of spiritual awakening and leadership are connected. The analogy of the oxygen masks dropping on a turbulent flight is similar to what we are talking about here: you need to be spiritually awake before you can become a great leader.

12 Symptoms of Spiritual Awakening

1. An increased tendency to let things happen rather than make them happen.
2. Frequent attacks of smiling.
3. Feelings of being connected with others and nature.
4. Frequent overwhelming episodes of appreciation.
5. A tendency to think and act spontaneously rather than from fears based on past experience.
6. An unmistakable ability to enjoy each moment.
7. A loss of ability to worry.
8. A loss of interest in conflict.
9. A loss of interest in interpreting the actions of others.
10. A loss of interest in judging others.
11. A loss of interest in judging self.
12. Gaining the ability to love without expecting anything.

http://recoverytradepublications.com/blog.html?entry=12-symptoms-of-a-spiritual

KINDNESS IS A LANGUAGE
WHICH THE DEAF CAN HEAR
AND THE BLIND CAN SEE.
-MARK TWAIN

Choose a positive mission for yourself, one that is moral and ethical. As I said, for me, it's volunteering at a soup kitchen; for you, it might be completely different— maybe joining Habitat for Humanity, reading to the aged or to children, or working with the families of our wounded warriors. Have a mission statement of exactly who you want to be as a leader. There is a great expression that says, "Lead, follow, or get out of the way." A leader not only has the ability to be in that 5 percent we talked about before but he or she also has the ability to bring other people into that fold and do good works. Mother Teresa said "that we cannot do great things in this world—we can only do small things with great love." And that is what I want you to do. Spend some time outside yourself; spend time helping the disadvantaged. I tried to do some charity work at a hospital for the aged. To be honest, it didn't work out. I was kind of freaked out about the whole thing. I cannot tell you why; it was just one of those things. But working in the soup kitchen was great. It was so rewarding to know that I was helping other people. *That* is what works for me. Figure out what works for you, but figure out how to become complete first. Only then you will have the ability to give back and pay it forward.

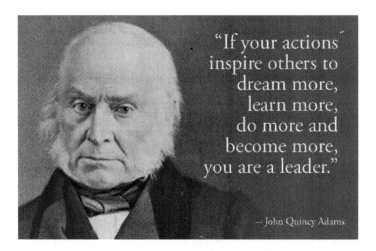

"If your actions inspire others to dream more, learn more, do more and become more, you are a leader."

-- John Quincy Adams

You've got to think big and be a team builder, and you've got to take risks. In this world, the only people who actually make it are the ones who take risks. We all live in a comfort circle, each one of us. That comfort circle is nice and warm. But if you want to succeed, you have to step outside that circle and take risks. That is the only way you can achieve great things. If you stay within that comfort circle, consider these words: "If you always do what you've always done, then you'll always get what you always got."

A leader is somebody who not only is committed but also has the ability to effectively communicate. You have to reach down and speak from the heart; that is really what effective communication is all about. That takes time, confidence, and practice.

I think it was Dale Carnage who said you can make friends faster in two weeks if you learn about them than if you talk about yourself for two years.

I want you to understand the needs, wants, and preferences of the other people before you start talking about yourself.

Be compassionate, be open, and be understanding. Go back to that chart—page 25—about the 95/5 rule. If you look down the second column (attributes of the 5 percent), those are all the qualities you need to be spiritually guided.

There will be times when somebody who is down (or coming in from the dark, as I say) wants to take you down as well. According to the law of attraction, if you are a *package* (someone who has it together), you will attract another person who is a package. And if you are a *project* (someone who needs a lot of work), you will attract a project.

Consider the quotation below that reads, "I did not cause it, so I can't cure it and I can't control it." There will be times when a person who is a project will be looking to you (a package) to be his or her enabler. Don't fall into this trap! Help others with compassion, understanding, and empathy, and give them a game plan, but then let them be accountable for their own actions.

> **I didn't cause it,
> so I can't control it
> and I can't cure it.**
> BETRACKS

My dear friends Robin Jay, Vicki Higgins, and John Assaraf are all friends with Don Miguel Ruiz, who wrote a great book called *The Four Agreements*. In summary, these "agreements" are as follows:

Be Impeccable with Your Word
Speak with integrity. Say only what you mean. Avoid using the word to speak against yourself or to gossip about others. Use the power of your word in the direction of truth and love.

Don't Take Anything Personally
Nothing others do is because of you. What others say and do is a projection of their own dream. When you are immune to the opinions and actions of others, you won't be the victim of needless suffering.

Don't Make Assumptions
Find the courage to ask questions and to express what you really want. Communicate with others as clearly as you can to avoid misunderstandings, sadness, and drama. With just this one agreement, you can completely transform your life.

Always Do Your Best
Your best is going to change from moment to moment; it will be different when you are healthy as opposed to sick. Under any circumstance, simply do your best and you will avoid self-judgment, self-abuse, and regret.

The Fitness Formula

As I mentioned earlier, a boss on Wall Street said to me, "If you can't put it on the back of your business card, don't bother telling me." So in the spirit of brevity, I will give you my Cliffs Notes on fitness and nutrition. I will share my secrets on fitness and nutrition and will cut to the chase.

If I had to sum up fitness in limited terms, I would start with my ten commandments:

1. Work out six days a week, but only to a 60 percent max level.
2. Know that diet is more important than the gym.
3. Get the majority of your calories in whole plant foods.
4. Eat four to five times a day—all small meals, and chew your food thirty-three times before swallowing.
5. Combine aerobic and anaerobic exercises.
6. Listen to upbeat music during your workout.
7. Reduce stress through meditation and quiet time.
8. Hydrate first thing when you wake up. Drink water with lemon.
9. Avoid sugar and salt as best you can.
10. Massage your feet during your morning shower (see page 101—Reflexology Chart in the Twenty-One-Day Action Plan on Day 1).

The second part of the fitness section is a compilation of articles on everything from calories to diabetes that I have collected over the years. Although I am not the author, I find them to have merit.

I have been into fitness for nearly fifty years, and many people have asked me to share my secrets. I say *secrets* because I have done and still can do what most people cannot do from a fitness perspective. Many of these feats can be seen on YouTube. For example, if you go to "Bill Morris's 10-20-30-40-50 workout," you will see what I accomplished in just under five minutes: ten pull-ups, twenty curls, thirty bar dips, forty sit-ups (with a forty-five-pound plate), and the tough one—fifty bench presses of my own weight (170 pounds).

If you go to www.billmorrisspeaker.com, you will see me minisquatting 840 pounds (five times my body weight).

As I mentioned earlier, the sit-up-athons I accomplished over five years for the Make-A-Wish Foundation, and now the potential of being a contestant on *The Next American Ninja Warrior*.

A famous line from *When Harry Met Sally* is, "I'll have what she's having." And that is what people want to know about me: What are my secrets?

Where to Begin

Well, before we get started, I would love for you to watch several documentaries that can be seen on Netflix:

- *Sugar Coated*
- *Cowspiracy*
- *Fat, Sick, and Nearly Dead*
- *Forks Over Knives*
- *Fed Up*
- *GMO OMG*
- *Hungry for Change*

I have always believed that getting educated is the foundation of the Formula for Success. To please my former boss, I'll keep it simple.

All food comes in only three categories: plant based, processed, and animal based.

If you get the majority (60–70 percent) of your caloric intake from plant-based whole foods, you are on your way to a healthy, successful life.

There is a great expression that says, "If it comes in a bag, box, can, bottle, jar, or package, you probably should avoid it." This is really tough, I know. What this means is you should avoid all aisles of the grocery store except the outside walls, where the fruits and vegetables are!

Why I Started with Nutrition

We are a very visual society, so many of you probably expected me to start the fitness discussion with aspects of body shaping or body imaging. After all, folks are interested in *how* I was able to achieve these fitness goals. Well, I started with nutrition because after all these years, I have come to the conclusion that 80 percent of fitness is what and how much we eat, and 20 percent is what we do in the gym.

Truth Be Told

Most people really do not comprehend the difference between a millionaire and a billionaire. It's simply outside their realm of understanding. The same is true for the idea of doing over twenty thousand consecutive sit-ups. When people ask me about my sit-up record, I always ask them to guess how many consecutive sit-ups I did, and 95 percent of the time, they guess between two hundred and a thousand!

As I mentioned in my YouTube video ("Bill Morris's 10-20-30-40-50 Workout"), I do 150 exercises in just under five minutes, listed below.

The 10-20-30-40-50 Workout
All done in five minutes!

10 pull-ups
20 curls (forty pounds in each hand)
30 bar dips
40 sit-ups holding a forty-five-pound Olympic plate
50 seated bench presses (using my body weight)

Watching someone do exercises for five minutes is, I admit, like watching paint dry. But have a look at what an old guy can do—something most people half my age cannot.

Over Time versus Overtime

Strength is developed over a long period of time by working overtime. When we were children, we wanted things immediately—what I call IG, or instant gratification. Unfortunately, some of us still have this desire.

In my Formula for Success, the section on goals should make things clear regarding how to achieve short- versus long-term goals. I believe you can be destroyed by being unrealistic. Think of the process as a marathon rather than a sprint.

When I use the word *overtime*, I mean just that: you have to do what others are not willing to do. Refer to the section on time management: you need to make the time—or at least reallocate the hours you have.

How Much Can You Bench?

For over twenty-five years, someone in my audience has asked me, "Bill, how much can you bench?"

First, I laugh hysterically because I knew the question was coming, and then I say, "Between seven and eight hundred pounds." Of course, this is a joke (and evidence of my warped sense of humor), but to see their faces is truly priceless. The truth is that I have never tried to max out.

My recommendation is to begin your fitness regime with light weights and more reps. Next, increase the weights appropriately over the years. Today, even as a T-Rex, I will use two seventy-pound dumbbells (one in each hand) and curl them twenty times. For sure, I did not start that way.

What Do You Eat?

Again, some people think there is something special I eat or a special supplement I take. There is not.

The next chapter contains articles written by people with expertise in areas of calories, vitamins, supplements, weight loss, carbs, super foods, diets, eating disorders, health tips and secrets, snacking, and sugar. I have included these articles because there is merit in them and some might be applicable to your personal situation. For example, if you have a particular deficiency, quite possibly a specific vitamin or supplement might be needed in your diet.

It seems there is sugar in 75 percent of all foods. To me, sugar is the devil. However, I am human, and on occasions, I will have a chocolate ice-cream bar. Let's be real. I don't beat myself up for this because I know it's not a regular part of my daily routine.

Key Secrets

I think some of the things that work for me can work for you as well. To begin with, I eat small portions. I think this is the fundamental first rule.

Second, I don't think twice about eating four or five times a day.

Third, I try to balance my carbs, protein, and fats (which we will talk about later). When I say *carbs*, there is a difference between simple and complex, and when I say *fats*, there is a difference between good fats and bad fats.

Yes, I drink coffee, and, yes, I always eat breakfast. I love having fish (except shellfish), salad, rice, vegetables, and one glass of wine for dinner. I try to avoid sugar and meat (although not 100 percent), and I *never* drink soda.

Regarding exercise, I work out daily, either in the gym or on a hike. If I am traveling—to see my sons, for instance—I will take off those days from the gym without guilt. Keep in mind: I have achieved a lot in fitness, so at this point, I am in more of a maintenance mode. In fact, the time I spend in the gym is less than half an hour a day (half anaerobic—lifting—and half aerobic—Stairmaster).

Let's look at today as the first day of the rest of your life. I say this because I sincerely hope the following information about fitness will motivate you to begin a new and healthy way of life: one that has you feeling better, reduces your stress, helps you to feel great about yourself (internally and externally), and encourages the desire to help others.

My daily workouts for you are fifteen to twenty-five minutes. Follow my instructions, and you will be able to get to a level of fitness that you could only dream about. The only thanks I want is for you to pay it forward and help another.

In the Twenty-One-Day Action Plan (page 93), I will start you off slowly—very slowly. This is because I want you to return every day to your workout. I want a new and improved way of life for you, and I want this to be like brushing your teeth: easy and routine.

There is no more important investment than you investing in you.

So let's start the fun. The first thing I want you to know is that from this day forward, this will be your new and improved way of life. What I mean by this is that you will be exercising *every* day of your life—and enjoying it! If you heed this advice, your newfound education about nutrition will make you feel wonderful physically.

I have always been a firm believer in the mind-body connection. Sure, I can get your body in shape and looking great, but unless the mind (mental part) is working in tandem with your workout (physical part), you will fail. What the mind can conceive, the body can achieve, so work them together.

Fitness: Great Articles

Over the years I have collected articles written by people with specific expertise regarding nutrition. After all, I think this is how we all learn. I have included several of these because they are all related to the Formula for Success. Although I have had nearly fifty years of learning, I am still learning.

So let's get started.

All about Calories

June 26, 2011 ("HealthDay News")—Curbing calories is the key ingredient for diabetics seeking to lose weight, and low-fat diets that are either high in protein *or* high in carbs are equally effective, researchers say.

"I think there are two key messages from this study," said study lead author Jeremy D. Krebs, a senior lecturer with the school of medicine and health sciences at the University of Otago in Wellington, New Zealand. "The first is that no matter what diet we prescribe, people find it extremely difficult to sustain the changes from their habitual diet over a long time. But if they are able to follow either a high-protein diet or a high-carbohydrate diet, they can achieve modest weight loss."

Krebs said this first message conveys flexibility and allows people to choose the approach that best suits them and "even to swap between dietary approaches when they get bored."

The second point "is that for people with diabetes, if they can adhere to either diet and achieve weight loss, then they do get benefits in terms of their diabetes control and cardiovascular risk," he added.

Krebs and his colleagues are scheduled to report their findings Sunday in San Diego at the American Diabetes Association meeting.

To compare the potential benefits of two popular dietetic approaches, the authors tracked nearly 300 overweight men and women between the ages of 35 and 75 who were on a new, two-year nutritional program.

To start, all the participants had a body mass index greater than 27, meaning they were moderately overweight, and all had type 2 diabetes.

The researchers randomly assigned the participants to one of two groups: a low-fat/high-protein group or a low-fat/high-carb group.

For the first half year, all attended twice-weekly group sessions led by a dietitian; for the following six months, sessions took place monthly.

Weight and waist circumference were measured at six months, one year, and two years. Kidney function and lipid (blood fats) profiles were also assessed throughout.

Food diaries indicated that total calorie intake went down in both groups. Ultimately, both groups lost a similar amount of weight and reduced their waist size in similar measure, the investigators found. And by the end of the two-year period, both groups had similar blood fat profiles.

Krebs and his colleagues concluded that their "real-world" experiment demonstrated that both approaches afford similar benefits, with the principal driving factor behind sustained weight loss being calorie reduction rather than either high-carb or high-protein consumption.

Lona Sandon, a registered dietitian and assistant professor of clinical nutrition at the University of Texas Southwestern Medical Center at Dallas, said the observations were "not at all surprising."

"This is pretty consistent with other research out there that has conducted other long-term comparisons in the general population," she said. "In the first six months you might see a little better benefit from a high-protein approach. But long-term, the initial benefits from a high-protein diet seem to diminish over time, and the two diets end up being essentially equivalent," Sandon explained.

"The bottom-line is that the issue for weight loss is calories," Sandon added. "Not where those calories come from. You need to create an energy deficit to lead to weight loss, and that happens by decreasing those calories. That's just been shown again and again."

Experts note that research presented at medical meetings is considered preliminary because it has not been subjected to the rigorous scrutiny required for publication in a peer-reviewed medical journal.

More information

For more on nutrition and diabetes, visit the American Diabetes Association.

What Are Trans Fats?

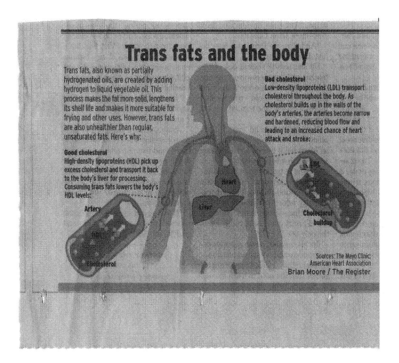

Trans fats and the body

Trans fats, also known as partially hydrogenated oils, are created by adding hydrogen to liquid vegetable oil. This process makes the fat more solid, lengthens its shelf life and makes it more suitable for frying and other uses. However, trans fats are also unhealthier than regular, unsaturated fats. Here's why:

Good cholesterol
High-density lipoproteins (HDL) pick up excess cholesterol and transport it back to the body's liver for processing. Consuming trans fats lowers the body's HDL levels.

Bad cholesterol
Low-density lipoproteins (LDL) transport cholesterol throughout the body. As cholesterol builds up in the walls of the body's arteries, the arteries become narrow and hardened, reducing blood flow and leading to an increased chance of heart attack and stroke.

Artery
Heart
Liver
LDL
Cholesterol buildup
HDL
Cholesterol

Sources: The Mayo Clinic;
American Heart Association
Brian Moore / The Register

Weight Gain Equals Bad Sleep

Women, try not to think of this if you lie awake at night: having trouble sleeping means you're likely to gain weight.

As if simply getting older weren't hard enough, new research shows that middle-aged and older women who have trouble falling or staying asleep may pack on more pounds than their well-rested contemporaries.

A number of studies have found that sleep-deprived children and adults are more likely to be overweight than those who usually get a full night's rest. But many of those studies assessed people at one point in time, so it was hard to know which came first, the sleep problems or the excess pounds.

A few studies have followed people over time, but they've disagreed about whether poor sleep is linked to expanding waistlines.

The new findings, reported in the International Journal of Obesity, strengthen the evidence that sleep problems are related to weight gain. In this case, the study design allowed the researchers to show that sleep problems came before substantial weight gain in some participants.

Finnish researchers followed more than 7,300 40- to 60-year-old adults for seven years. They found that women who reported significant sleep problems at the outset generally put on more weight over time than women who slept well.

Roughly one-third of women with frequent sleep problems gained at least 11 pounds, versus about a fifth of women with no sleep difficulties at the outset.

Men were spared, however. Their sleep problems were not related to weight gain.

The link in the women persisted even when the investigators accounted for a number of factors that can affect both sleep quality and weight gain—including participants' body weight at the study's start, their exercise habits and their general physical and mental health.

While the findings do not prove cause-and-effect, they raise the possibility that improving sleep quality might help stave off excess weight gain, lead researcher Peppi Lyytikainen, of the University of Helsinki, told Reuters Health by e-mail.

The 7,332 men and women in the study were first surveyed between 2000 and 2002. Those who said they'd had trouble falling asleep or staying asleep on at least 14 nights in the past month were classified as having "frequent" sleep problems. The study participants also reported their weight and height during the first survey, then again five to seven years later.

At the outset, 20 percent of women had frequent sleep problems. Overall, the study found, those women were more likely to report a "major" weight gain—11 pounds or more—by the study's end compared to women who slept well.

But the 17 percent of men who reported sleep problems were no more likely to gain weight than those who slept without difficulty.

The reason for the disparate findings for men and women is unclear, according to Lyytikainen's team. But it might be related to the fact that the study included a smaller number of men than women—1,300 versus more than 5,700—which may have made any potential effect among men harder to detect.

This type of study, however—in which researchers observe people over time—can't prove cause-and-effect. While the researchers accounted for a number of variables related to sleep and weight—like self-reported general health and exercise and other lifestyle habits—they cannot rule out the possibility that factors other than sleep problems account for the higher risk of substantial weight.

Other research does suggest that sleep deprivation may affect the body in ways that contribute to weight gain, Lyytikainen said.

There is evidence, for example, that sleep loss alters people's levels of the appetite-regulating hormones leptin and ghrelin—which could, in theory, spur them to overeat.

It is unknown, however, whether treating insomnia and other sleep disturbances has any added benefit for people's waistlines. SOURCE:

http://link.reuters.com/nub45m *International Journal of Obesity*, online June 8, 2010.

Hydration: Water versus Coke
WATER

- #1. 75% of Americans are chronically dehydrated. (also applies to half the world population)
- #2. In 37% of Americans, the thirst mechanism is so weak that it is mistaken for hunger.
- #3. Even MILD dehydration will slow down one's metabolism as much as 3%.
- #4. One glass of water will shut down midnight hunger pangs for almost 100% of the dieters studied in a University of Washington study.
- #5. Lack of water, the #1 trigger of daytime fatigue.
- #6. Preliminary research indicates that 8–10 glasses of water a day could significantly ease back and joint pain for up to 80% of sufferers.
- #7. A mere 2% drop in body water can trigger fuzzy short-term memory, trouble with basic math, and difficulty focusing on the computer screen or on a printed page.
- #8. Drinking 5 glasses of water daily decreases the risk of colon cancer by 45%, plus it can slash the risk of breast cancer by 79% and one is 50% less likely to develop bladder cancer.

Are you drinking the amount of water you should drink every day?

COKE

- #1. In many states the highway patrol carries two gallons of Coke in the trunk to remove blood from the highway after a car accident.
- #2. You can put a T-bone steak in a bowl of Coke and it will be gone in two days.
- #3. To clean a toilet: Pour a can of Coca-Cola into the toilet bowl and let the "real thing" sit for one hour, then flush clean. The citric acid in Coke removes stains from vitreous china.

#4. To remove rust spots from chrome car bumpers:
Rub the bumper with a rumpled-up piece of Reynolds Wrap aluminum foil dipped in Coca-Cola.

#5. To clean corrosion from car battery terminals:
Pour a can of Coca-Cola over the terminals to bubble away the corrosion.

#6. To loosen a rusted bolt:
Apply a cloth soaked in Coca-Cola to the rusted bolt for several minutes.

#7. To bake a moist ham: Empty a can of Coca-Cola into the baking pan, wrap the ham in aluminum foil, and bake.
Thirty minutes before ham is finished, remove the foil, allowing the drippings to mix with the Coke for a sumptuous brown gravy.

#8. To remove grease from clothes:
Empty a can of Coke into the load of greasy clothes, add detergent, and run through a regular cycle. The Coca-Cola will help loosen grease stains. It will also clean road haze from your windshield.

FOR YOUR INFORMATION

#1. The active ingredient in Coke is phosphoric acid. It will dissolve a nail in about four days. Phosphoric acid also leaches calcium from bones and is a major contributor to the rising increase of osteoporosis.

#2. To carry Coca-Cola syrup (the concentrate) the commercial trucks must use a hazardous Material place cards reserved for highly corrosive materials.

#3. The distributors of Coke have been using it to clean engines of the trucks for about 20 years!
Now the question is, would you like a glass of water?

Veggies

Is it healthier to eat raw veggies or to cook them? Is fresh broccoli more nutritious than frozen? Is eating iceberg lettuce a waste of time?

You may be surprised by the answers to these seemingly simple questions. In fact, there are several misconceptions when it comes to vegetables. The one universal truth is that most of us could be eating more of them.

As summer approaches, we have more vegetable choices than at any other time of year. Here's a guide to what's fact and what's fiction when it comes to eating your veggies.

Myth: Fresh vegetables are more nutritious than frozen

Fact: Studies show that sometimes you can get more nutrients from frozen veggies, depending on variety and how old the vegetables at your supermarket are. That's because produce starts losing nutrient quality as soon as it's picked.

Frozen vegetables are flash-frozen right after harvest so they are preserved at their peak of freshness when they are most nutritious. Your best bet in terms of taste, nutrition, and the environment is still local in-season produce. When that's not an option frozen can be a better choice (from a nutrient standpoint) than spinach that takes two weeks to reach your table.

Myth: Cooked veggies are less nutritious than raw

Fact: It depends on the vegetable. "Cooking destroys some nutrients, but it releases others," says Marion Nestle, author of "What to Eat". It destroys vitamin C and folic acid, according to Nestle, which is why it's not a great idea to cook oranges.

On the other hand, she says, cooking releases vitamin A and the nutrients in fiber and makes them easier to digest. It's also easier for your body to absorb more lycopene, a cancer-fighting antioxidant, in cooked tomato sauce than from raw tomatoes.

Steam or roast veggies instead of boiling, which leaches out water-soluble vitamins into the cooking water.

Myth: Iceberg lettuce doesn't have any nutrients

Fact: Iceberg lettuce is mostly water so it's hardly loaded with vitamins, but a large head does contain small amounts of protein, fiber, vitamins, and minerals.

You'll get more nutrients from other greens that have less water such as romaine or butter head lettuce, but contrary to popular belief, iceberg lettuce does have some nutritional value.

Myth: Local vegetables are always cheaper

Fact: It's certainly true that local produce can be good for your budget. This is especially true during the peak of harvest when farmers need to get rid of an abundant crop and there is a lot of competition.

However, there are no guarantees. Local food "is not in any way subsidized so you are paying the real cost of producing the food, and the economies of scale are not there," says Nestle.

Some tips for finding the best deals at your local farmers' market: Shop at the end of the day when farmers are likely to mark down their prices in order to get rid of their inventory. (Go early in the day if selection is more important than price.) Ask your farmer for a volume discount if he or she doesn't already offer one. Take advantage of special deals on bruised or overripe veggies. Prices vary from farmer to farmer so shop around before buying.

Myth: Potatoes make you fat

Fact: Potatoes are virtually fat-free and low in calories. These delicious and inexpensive root vegetables contain a healthy dose of fiber, which can actually make you feel satisfied for longer and help you lose weight.

It's not the potatoes themselves that make you fat. It's how you cook them and what you slather on your spuds that can cause you to pack on the pounds.

Myth: Bagged salads are squeaky clean

Fact: They're not nearly as clean as you may think. Consumer Reports tests found bacteria that are "common indicators of poor sanitation and fecal contamination" in 39 percent of the 208 packages of salad greens it tested. It didn't find E. coli 0157:H7, listeria, or other disease-causing bacteria in its samples.

But it's still a good idea to give greens a good rinse to remove residual soil before eating even if the bag says they're "prewashed" or "triple-washed."

Myth: Farmer's markets only have organics

Fact: Just because a vegetable (or anything for that matter) is sold at a farmers' market does not mean that it's organic. It still must be certified organic by the US Department of Agriculture for a guarantee that it was grown without synthetic fertilizers and pesticides.

Some farmers will say they are in the process of getting certified, they grow crops without synthetic chemicals but can't afford the certification process, or they only use chemicals when they have no choice and don't use them when it's close to harvest time. It's your call on whether you trust that farmer.

Environmental journalist Lori Bongiorno shares green-living tips and product reviews with Yahoo! Green's users. Send Lori a question or suggestion for potential use in a future column. Her book, Green Greener Greenest: A Practical Guide to Making Eco-smart Choices a Part of Your Life *is available on Yahoo! Shopping and Amazon.com.*

Diabetes
Diabetes Rate Doubles

The number of adults with diabetes worldwide has more than doubled since 1980, with almost 350 million now affected, according to a new study published in "The Lancet" medical journal.

Scientists from Imperial College London and Harvard University analyzed blood sugar of 2.7 million people aged 25 and over across the world and used the results to estimate diabetes prevalence.

The number of adults with diabetes more than doubled from 153 million in 1980 to 347 million in 2008, according to the research published Saturday.

Diabetes is caused by poor blood sugar control and can lead to heart disease and stroke and can damage the kidneys, nerves and eyes.

High blood sugar levels and diabetes kill three million people across the world each year.

The researchers said two of the strongest factors in the rising diabetes rate were increasing life span and body weight, especially among women.

"Our study has shown that diabetes is becoming more common almost everywhere in the world," said Majid Ezzati, from Imperial College London, who co-led the study.

"This is in contrast to blood pressure and cholesterol, which have both fallen in many regions. Diabetes is much harder to prevent and treat than these other conditions."

Diabetes rates had risen most in Pacific island nations, where a greater proportion of people have the condition than anywhere else in the world, according to the study.

In the Marshall Islands, one in three women and one in four men has diabetes, it found.

Countries in Western Europe had seen a relatively small increase in diabetes prevalence

8 Foods That Help You Live Longer
Load up on health-boosting super foods that combat breast cancer, heart disease and more.

By Alexandra Gekas

If you're tired of reading about must-eat super foods that are hard to find—and even harder to pronounce; (hello, açai berry and quinoa)—take heart: Your pantry

THE FORMULA FOR SUCCESS

may hold more super powered wonders than you realize! From chocolate and coffee to red wine and walnuts, the following eight amazing everyday foods can help improve your health.

Chocolate

Good news for all the chocoholics out there: Cocoa just might be one of the heart-healthiest foods around! A 2011 Harvard study found that organic compounds called flavonoids that are contained in cacao (the bean used to make chocolate) are associated with reduced blood pressure as well as improved blood vessel health, cholesterol levels and general blood flow. "All of these things are protective against heart disease," says Eric Ding, PhD, conductor of the study and a professor of nutrition and epidemiology at the Harvard School of Public Health. "But the HDL findings—the increase in good cholesterol—nobody knew about that until our study, as well as the improved blood flow." As good as that news is, it's not a green light to eat any and every chocolate bar you come across. "Eighty percent of the chocolate we consume in this country is not healthy," says Joseph Maroon, MD, professor of neurosurgery at the University of Pittsburgh and author of _The Longevity Factor_. "It's pure sugar and doesn't have the flavonoids in it from the original cacao tree and bean." The experts we spoke to recommend snacking on two to four squares per day of dark chocolate that has at least 70% to 75% cacao, because it has more flavonoids. If you're not a chocolate fan, Dr. Ding and Dr. Maroon both recommend taking a 400 to 450 mg cocoa flavonoid supplement in lieu of eating squares.

Coffee

While coffee has been widely touted for its health benefits, a recent study amounted to a small victory for male coffee drinkers. According to a 2011 Harvard study, coffee consumption has been linked to decreased rates of prostate cancer. In the study, men who drank six or more cups of coffee per day were found to have a 20% lower risk of developing prostate cancer and a 60% lower risk of developing lethal prostate cancer, according to researcher Lorelei Mucci, PhD, study author and associate professor of epidemiology at the Harvard School of Public Health. "We saw the same lower risk whether the men only drank decaf, only drank caffeinated or drank both, so it's something other than the caffeine," Dr. Mucci says. Though downing six cups of joe every day is probably too much for most people, rest assured that the study still found lower rates of prostate cancer in men who only drank one to three cups per day, compared to those who drank none at all. Get him in the habit by making a double batch when enjoying your morning brew.

Watercress

While it may not be the most popular leafy green, watercress has been associated with one very positive health impact for women: It may inhibit the growth of breast cancer tumors. Though only a small study was conducted, scientists at England's University of Southampton reported in 2011 that a compound in watercress can "turn off" the signal that sends blood flow to a tumor, in essence stopping the tumor in its tracks. "All cancers develop new blood vessels, so if you interfere with the development of new blood vessels, you effectively impede the blood supply to the tumor," Dr. Maroon says. "A lot of the drugs [that treat breast cancer] prevent the tumors from making new blood vessels, and in that way, can slow, impede or eradicate the growth of some tumors." Although more research is needed, it's safe to assume that adding this leafy green to your diet, whether as a sandwich topping or in salads, couldn't hurt.

Walnuts

Most nuts are recognized as super foods, thanks to a high concentration of unsaturated fatty acids, like omega-3s, which help lower cholesterol and decrease the risk of heart disease. However, a 2011 study indicates that walnuts might be the most super nut of them all. According to study author Joe Vinson, PhD, professor of chemistry at Scranton University in Pennsylvania, walnuts contain twice the amount of antioxidants per ounce as peanuts and almonds, two popular types of nuts consumed in the United States. His research found that all nuts in general were better sources of antioxidants when compared to pure vitamin E (a type of antioxidant). But when walnuts were compared to peanuts and almonds, they were found to be better in terms of the "quality and quantity of antioxidants." According to Kari Kooi, RD, corporate wellness dietitian at The Methodist Hospital in Houston, that means walnuts can not only help improve cholesterol levels but also help manage your weight by providing satisfying heart-healthy fats and protein.

Olive Oil

Olive oil has long been associated with the heart-healthy Mediterranean diet, but it may benefit more than just your ticker. In a 2011 study, researchers analyzed the olive oil consumption of 7,625 French people 65 or older and found that those whose use of olive oil was "intensive" were 41% less likely to suffer a stroke compared with those who never consumed olive oil. "We can't infer which aspects of olive oil may prevent stroke," says study author Cécilia Samieri, PhD, a professor of epidemiology and nutrition at the University of Bordeaux in France. However, Dr. Samieri says, it's possible that the oleic acid in olive oil decreases the absorption of saturated fats—and, ultimately, the chance of stroke.

Apples

It looks like an apple a day really can keep the doctor away—especially when it comes to heart health. A 2011 study conducted by researchers at Florida State University compared postmenopausal women who ate 75 grams of dried apple a day to women who ate other types of dried fruit. The result? Women who ate the dried apple saw a 23% drop in their LDL ("bad") cholesterol, as well as a 4% increase in their HDL ("good") cholesterol. What's more, the additional 240 calories derived from the dried apple slices didn't cause participants to gain weight—the apple group actually lost an average of 3.3 lbs over the course of the year in which the study was conducted. Although dried apples were used in the study, eating the equivalent amount of fresh apples is believed to produce similar results.

Whole Grains

New research may make you think twice before buying that loaf of white bread. Foods that contain whole grains and bran, like stone-ground whole-grain bread, brown rice and old-fashioned oatmeal, can help protect against coronary heart disease and aid in digestive health. They also improve insulin sensitivity, which can help better control your sugar levels—a vital factor for diabetics. A 2010 study found that the intake of whole grains was associated with a 16 to 31% overall reduction in the risk of dying from any cause in participants with type 2 diabetes. "Whole grains can slow the absorption of cholesterol, just like some of the drugs that you take [for high cholesterol] do," says Dr. Maroon. In essence, by improving your overall cholesterol count, you can help lower your risk of heart disease.

Red Wine

What could be better than chocolate being good for you? Red wine! (In moderation, of course.) According to a 2011 report from the University of Florida, which reviewed several studies on resveratrol—a polyphenol compound that is naturally found in red wine—it may have "anti-aging, anti-carcinogenic, anti-inflammatory and antioxidant properties." It is important to note that the studies were conducted on laboratory animals, but there is plenty of anecdotal evidence to support the claim. The key is in the polyphenols, which Dr. Maroon says, "can reduce inflammation…increase HDL and lower LDL [cholesterol levels], have a mild to modest effect on blood pressure, dilate blood vessels to improve blood flow to the brain and heart, and lower insulin resistance," which helps prevent type 2 diabetes. However, that doesn't mean you can drink a bottle of wine every night with dinner. "I don't encourage people to drink alcohol who haven't in the past [or who suffer from alcoholism]," says Dr. Maroon. "What I do say is one glass of wine for women and no more than two for men [per day] is healthy." Though wine is no fountain of youth, it can help delay the body's aging process.

The Twenty-One-Day Action Plan

Much has been written on the characteristics, desires, and goals of the past three generations—baby boomers (born after 1945 and through 1961), gen Xers (born between 1961 and 1980), and millennials (born between 1980 and 1996). Although there are distinct differences among generations, one thing that is not different is the Formula for Success.

Before I begin teaching a class at the Paul Merage School of Business (whether it's undergraduates or MBA students), I test the students to see how much they really know about business. I don't want to talk over their heads or below their knowledge base. Likewise, this twenty-one-day plan will not be complex, but it will cover the basics and create a routine that will help you in the years ahead.

Former Wall Street executive, world-class athlete, corporate executive, serial entrepreneur, top-business-school professor—these are some of the accolades I have been given, and every achievement started with a plan of action as well as definable goals.

My personal belief is that all accomplishments—big or small—start with a plan of action. This twenty-one-day action plan is designed to (1) give you structure toward accomplishments and (2) have you achieve small goals that will serve as the foundation for larger goals. This isn't a one-size-fits-all solution. After all, we all have different strengths and weakness, and we all have different starting points.

In my world, to be a better you, a leader, or simply a goal-oriented achiever, you have to be at the service of others. What this means is that it's not all about you! I know that sounds somewhat odd when we are talking about *your* twenty-one-day action plan. Well, when you discover exactly how this works, you will understand.

Think of success as a two-phase accomplishment. The first phase is about you. Yes, you have to have it together before you can help another. The second phase is to be able to help another once you are ready. Success only comes to those who have completed *both* phases. In the paragraph above regarding the accolades others have bestowed upon me, what is more important to me is what I recognize about myself. I hope that when I complete the second phase, I am recognized as a great father and an accomplished life coach to you.

This formula is all about how to get your life in balance and achieve some fabulous goals that you will set just for you. It is how to get it together mentally, physically, and spiritually.

If an athlete approaches me and asks for my help in getting to the next level, I first need to do an assessment of where he or she is before I begin training. Second, I design a plan of action that starts out slow and then ramps up. So it will be for you in your twenty-one-day action plan.

Inasmuch as I don't know where you are now—whether you are a young man or woman, are working or going to school, need to gain weight or lose weight, and so on—I will make the plan somewhat generic and ramp you up slowly. I believe it's basic human nature to want success right away. Unfortunately, success doesn't work that way. It's a process. It's a formula. It's repetition. It's consistency. It's routine. And it's achieved through proper construction of your belief system.

Let's Get Started
Day 1
Mental

First comes time management. I want you to divide your twenty-four-hour day up as it happens now. For example, the components might be sleeping, eating, playing, working, reading, working out, or helping others.

Be sure the hours add up to twenty-four, and then determine how many hours you believe are an investment in your future and how many hours are, in financial terms, a withdrawal or an expense. In other words, how many hours are not moving you toward your goals and are, as such, a waste of time? Of course, a balanced person needs some downtime, so don't feel all your time has to be "invested."

Physical

Examine the past year of your life. Have you gained weight or lost weight? Maybe you weighed 150 pounds last year, and today you weigh 160 pounds. If this is the case, then it simply means you are consuming more calories than you are burning off. If you now weigh 140 pounds, then the opposite is true. Get an estimate of the calories you consume daily. I also want you to massage your feet while taking your morning shower. While standing, I take my right foot and rest it on my left knee, and then I switch legs. Do this every day!

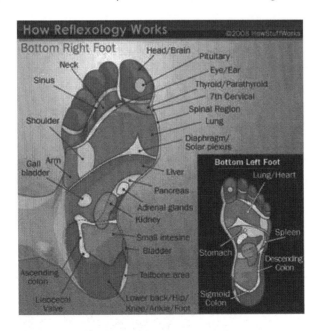

Spiritual

I want you to compliment two people today—and be sincere. Also I want you to help somebody with a project he or she has been struggling with.

The aforementioned tasks (mental, physical, and spiritual) should take about five minutes each.

Day 2

Mental

Now that you have broken down your time, examine the hours you identified as spending and those you identified as investing. Proper time management is critical and important for success, so let's allocate two hours to investing from an area where you are now spending. For example, reading is an investment, so take an hour from the spending column, shut off your phone (and I don't just mean putting it on silent), and read for twenty-one minutes.

Physical

Starting today I want you to do two things that you will do for the rest of this twenty-one-day period. The first is to stop drinking soda, and the second is to drink water (at least one sixteen-ounce-bottle in the morning and another in the afternoon). I also want you to test yourself to see how many push-ups and sit-ups you can do. For argument sake, let's say you can do ten push-ups and ten sit-ups. I want you to start tomorrow doing 30 percent of your maximum, so if today you max out at ten, tomorrow you will do three of each.

A week from now, increase that percentage to 50 percent (or five of each), and a week from that, increase to 60 percent (or 6 of each) for each of the remaining days.

Also, when you are eating meals, take your time. Be sure to chew each bite thirty-three times, and eat small meals four or five times a day.

Spiritual

I want you to research the various charities in your area—you should be able to come up with at least a dozen—and pick one at which to become a volunteer.

Day 3
Mental
Today I want you to start working on your goals. Break them down into short- and long-term goals. A short-term goal is what you want to accomplish in a year. For our twenty-one-day plan, you will concentrate on these.

You might be saying, "Where do I start?" Well, think about the future you see yourself in. Identify your passions first—that will help you pick the field of endeavor. Let's say you are inclined to be a plumber or an electrician. If that's the case, then map out the education you will need to acquire over the next several years. Let nothing get in your way. The first time you write your goals, it will feel odd, and revisions will happen, but it is the actual writing of them that creates realism—not dreams.

Physical
Continue with your push-ups and sit-ups, and now incorporate some walking. Ideally, you should walk a mile (if you are capable). Be sure to stay hydrated! Drink plenty of water, and go at a leisurely pace.

Spiritual
Make some phone calls to see which charities are accepting volunteers. Keep a list and a log of the conversations.

Day 4
Mental
Today I want you to list what you believe are setbacks (not failures) that you have experienced over the past year. Examine them, and understand that these are things you no longer have any control over—they happened in the past. However, you can create closure and, more importantly, learn from them. For example, if someone did you wrong and this prevented you from achieving a specific objective, forgive that person. This is not easy, but it will free you up for future success. It's been said that for every sixty seconds of bottled-up anger inside you, you lose a minute of happiness!

Physical

I want you to see a documentary today called *Sugar Coated*. Also, continue with your push-ups and sit-ups workout.

Spiritual

Regarding the charity you will volunteer with, I want you to enlist a friend to work with you. Hopefully, you will not only help the less fortunate but also influence a friend on the journey.

Day 5

Mental

In your time-management chart (spending versus investing), I want you to take an hour that you feel you were spending and convert that hour to investing, even if it's doing research on future educational courses.

Physical

Today I want you to see the documentary *Fat, Sick, and Nearly Dead* and continue your workout regimen.

Spiritual

Today I want you to go out of your way to help someone. This can be anything, from just being there for a friend to helping someone with a task like homework.

Day 6

Mental

Today I want you to create your own personal "goal card" and carry it wherever you go. It should be the size of a credit card or slightly larger. I also want you to create a similar list and attach it to your lamp near your bed so it's the last thing you see when you go to sleep and the first thing you see when you wake up.

Physical

Keep it simple, and keep up with your push-ups and sit-ups. Walk a mile, continue to drink water, and make sure there is *no* soda in your life. When you take a shower in the morning, massage the bottoms of both feet. Put the right foot just above the kneecap of the left leg, and take your thumb and massage the bottom of the foot for about twenty-one seconds. Then do the opposite foot. Search *Chinese foot massage* online to see the organs that are related to the various spots on the foot (see page 96).

Spiritual

Today I want you to pay it forward. Find something you are very good at, and share it with someone. For example, if you are good in math, tutor someone.

Day 7

Mental

This completes one week of your new journey. Review your time-management chart and the goals you have established. Then spend some time going over what I call PMA, or positive mental attitude. Focus on the positive aspects of making success happen, and be grateful for all you have.

Physical

I want you to learn about calories by watching a Netflix documentary called *Forks over Knives*. And, of course, keep up with your fitness regimen! Remember, I want you at every meal to chew your food thirty-three times. Yes, meals will take a little longer, but the good news is that your stomach won't have to work so hard to break down the food consumed.

Spiritual

Connect with your higher power. Shut off your phone, and spend an hour meditating. This will seem odd at first and very quiet, but give it a shot for fifteen minutes.

For the next two weeks, I want you to repeat this seven-day exercise until your mind, body, and spirit are aligned with your time management and your goals. By day twenty-one, you will be on track for great things and amazing improvement.

SUMMARY

We as human beings need three things—hope, love, and having a sense of purpose.

HOPE
I sincerely hope that the guidelines and concepts in this book will give you the opportunity to create and execute your personal goals and have-*The Formula for Success.*

When you hone in on your new time management and link it with your new found goals, you will be on your way. Dealing with setbacks is another key that will allow you the ability to "unlock your potential." Always remember we all have many more setbacks than successes; deal with them and learn from them, and embrace the journey.

LOVE
I would like to share a little love story. Remember I said the Formula for Success isn't about the accumulation of money. I believe it is the accumulation of love, whether you are rich or poor monetarily—connect with love.

Poor Man...or...Rich Man
A very poor man lived with his wife. One day, his wife, who had very long hair, asked him to buy her a comb for her hair to grow well and to be well groomed.

The man felt very sorry and said no. He explained that he did not even have enough money to fix the strap of his watch he had just broken.

She did not insist on her request.

The man went to work and passed by a watch shop, sold his damaged watch at a low price, and went to buy a comb for his wife.

He came home in the evening with the comb in his hand ready to give to his wife.

He was surprised when he saw his wife with a very short haircut.

She had sold her hair and was holding a new watch band.

Tears flowed simultaneously from their eyes, not for the futility of their actions, but for the reciprocity of their love.

MORAL: To love is nothing, to be loved is something, but to love and to be loved by the one you love, that is EVERYTHING. Never take love for granted.

Sense of Purpose

Like our fingerprints, we are all unique. Find your personal "road to happy" by converting your passion into your own "mission statement."

The most important asset we have is our time. I think the following story will make you think about that.

The Last Wishes Of Alexander the Great

On his deathbed, Alexander summoned his generals and told them his three ultimate wishes.

1. The best doctors should carry his coffin,
2. The wealth he had accumulated (money, gold, precious stones) should be scattered along the way to his burial, and
3. His hands should be left hanging outside the coffin for all to see.

Surprised by these unusual requests, one of his generals asked Alexander to explain. Here is what he said:

1. I want the best doctors to carry my coffin to demonstrate that in the face of death, even the best doctors in the world have no power to heal.
2. I want the road to be covered with my treasure so that everybody sees that the wealth acquired on earth stays on earth.
3. I want my hands to swing in the wind so that people understand that we come to this world empty-handed and we leave empty-handed after the most precious treasure of all is exhausted—time.

Time is our most precious treasure because it is limited. We can produce more wealth, but we cannot produce more time.

When we give someone our time, we actually give a portion of our life that we will never take back. Our time is our life!

I believe the best present I can give you is the time I put into this book, to help you on your journey toward success and the "Road to Happy."

The best present you can give your family and friends is your time. May you have the wisdom to give it now that you have the Formula for Success.

God Bless.

Made in the USA
San Bernardino, CA
04 February 2020